HOT TIMES DURING THE COLD WAR

HOT TIMES DURING THE COLD WAR

AN AMERICAN COMES OF AGE IN WEST GERMANY

SCOTT W. HAWLEY

iUniverse, Inc.
New York Lincoln Shanghai

Hot Times During the Cold War
An American Comes of Age in West Germany

Copyright © 2007 by Scott W. Hawley

All rights reserved. No part of this book may be used or reproduced by any means, graphic, electronic, or mechanical, including photocopying, recording, taping or by any information storage retrieval system without the written permission of the publisher except in the case of brief quotations embodied in critical articles and reviews.

iUniverse books may be ordered through booksellers or by contacting:

iUniverse
2021 Pine Lake Road, Suite 100
Lincoln, NE 68512
www.iuniverse.com
1-800-Authors (1-800-288-4677)

Because of the dynamic nature of the Internet, any Web addresses or links contained in this book may have changed since publication and may no longer be valid.

The views expressed in this work are solely those of the author and do not necessarily reflect the views of the publisher, and the publisher hereby disclaims any responsibility for them.

ISBN: 978-0-595-44233-1 (pbk)
ISBN: 978-0-595-88563-3 (ebk)

Printed in the United States of America

To the sons and daughters
of American military personnel,
fellow nomads
from everywhere and nowhere.

Contents

Acknowledgments . . . . *xi*
Preface . . . . *xiii*

Arrival 1
Transatlantic 2
Piccadilly Circus 4
Bomb Threat 5
Base Commander's Son 7
Tunnel Rats 9

Daily Grind 11
Sand Pits 12
Base Exchange 13
Expectations 14
Look Behind You 15
Libya 17
Bush 18
Movie Night 20
Back Gate 21

School Days 23
English Teacher 24
Pea Head 26
Greased Buns 28
Creative Writing 29

Angela *31*
The Frau *33*
Autobahn *35*
Lonely *37*
Friend *38*
Cock Watcher *39*
Say What? *40*
Bad Kisser *41*
Skeet *42*
Dinner *43*
Courting *45*
Finally *46*

L.O.S.T. 49
L.O.S.T. *50*
Joe D'Ionra *51*
Eric the Bassist *52*
Pickles *53*
Toenail *54*
Hardcore *55*
New Line-Up *56*
Prom Night *58*

Hitting the Road 59
Goggles *60*
Haircut *62*
Meet and Greet *64*
Digging *65*
Butt Lint *66*
Andorra *67*

Ugly American 69
Dutch Ducks 70
Homesick 71
Auf Wiedersehen 73

Acknowledgments

I am grateful for the copy editing skills of Valerie Davis and the editing skills of Karen Schrier.

Most of all, I would like to thank my wife, Portia, for her tireless support and encouragement. I could not have done this without her.

PREFACE

From 1985 to 1988, I lived on Rhein Main Air Force Base, a bustling U.S. military installation located in the heart of what was then West Germany. The son of an Air Force officer, I attended Frankfurt American High School, one of six hundred children of U.S. military personnel.

While we studied calculus and chemistry and sold candy bars to get the track team to Brussels, our parents commanded tank battalions, flew transport aircraft, and honed their combat skills.

Despite coming of age in a community preparing for Armageddon, we reveled in the wondrous cacophony of stoners, drama geeks, skaters, letter-jacket athletes, and break-dancers. The energy generated from the collisions and collaborations of these groups burned brighter than a thousand suns.

Arrival

TRANSATLANTIC

On the pulpy orange-juice morning
we left America to begin life abroad,

>I perched for a moment
>at the top of the ramp
>in my friend's backyard,
>in the neighborhood I knew,
>full of people I liked,
>>and went for it—

and fell hard off my skateboard
to land in Maggie Thatcher's London,
with screeching runway wheels
and passengers who spoke funny languages,
who pretended to look away
while I blew chunks into the air-sickness bag.

But that was nothing compared to
spitting greasy bile down the side
of the boxy black taxi,

>*dry heaving*

with my head out the window,
while the driver clenched his teeth
and called me "mate,"
and my parents smiled awkwardly,

as we NATO allies
rode together

on the wrong side of the road
to the hotel.

PICCADILLY CIRCUS

Thousands of miles from home
we opened a guidebook
and circled names like Buckingham Palace
and Trafalgar Square,
speculating on who would spy
    a double-
    decker bus,
a bobby,

    a red
    phone
    booth,
a Beatle,

    or even King Arthur himself.

But we were woefully unprepared
as we stepped from the hotel,
squeaky, American, innocent,
and spotted an English hobo
(*He looks a lot like ours.*)
tucked into an alley,
(*What's he doing?*)
having a jolly good time,
(*Don't look ... I said, don't look! Keep moving ...*)
fishing his chip.

BOMB THREAT

We played leapfrog over froggy France
and landed in the breech,
where East and West
played high-stakes chicken
with armies sharpened for slaughter.

And we raced to the safety
of Rhein Main

and its barbed wire,
    attack dogs,
        water cannons,
            and M-16s,

only to be jolted awake
and herded down
the fire escape away from the building,
(Away from the building!)
wearing bathrobes
and middle-of-the-night
pajamas with dozens
of other Americans just in country.

And after asking about hometowns,
and joking about duty assignments,
we murmured to each other
upon learning
the Red Army Faction had
spirited a People's Wagon
full of explosives

past the barbed wire,
    attack dogs,
        water cannons,
            and M-16s,

and *slam-kablasted* the front off
base headquarters,
killing two airmen
not five minutes before our
own rude awakening.

BASE COMMANDER'S SON

As the sun set orange, pink, and yellow,
I lunged for a pass
and muddied my tighty-whities
but didn't let on,
because I had just met David.

I told him I was thirsty and walked
carefully into his cream-colored
stucco stairwell, past the
(Can they smell it?)
adults sipping cocktails,
eating peanuts,
telling grown-up stories
with grown-up chuckles
and nods and frowns,
until I found the bathroom
to clean myself up.

But there was no saving the underwear,
which I rolled slowly into a small, white ball,

working carefully,
    like a submarine commander,

stuffing the torpedo into the chrome plumbing
        underneath the sink,
        back in the far back,
        where the main pipe
        makes a sharp turn.

Then I prayed
that in a couple of days,

after the cocktails wore off
and the peanuts passed,
the base commander
and his charming wife
would think the stink bomb
belonged to David.

TUNNEL RATS

Having—*adrenaline rush!*—stumbled
onto forgotten tunnels
in the foundation of the stairwell,
we explored each new passageway
like we were sneaking into Moscow,
crawling slowly
        (just barely)
on bellies that got ground-in filthy-dirty,
before emerging one building over,
gulping for air in an unsuspecting laundry room
(after stopping halfway to hide
a *Penthouse* and burn our names
into the walls, in case we never got out).

Until some do-gooder,
never-had-fun-in-her-life mom
heard we were underground
burning things and looking at porn,
and the security teams came without warning
one day in big blue utility trucks
to seal the tunnels with thick
steel doors. *For our own good,* they said.

The bastards.

Daily Grind

SAND PITS

Outside Rhein Main, in the woods past the barbed wire,
we used bare hands to dig caves on hot summer days,
in the sandy walls of an old quarry.
Then we climbed inside, where it was cool,
to talk about the States,
    and the people we'd left behind,
    and the places we'd once called home,
wondering out loud if Ivan *really* had it out for us,
before crawling out to throw rocks into the turquoise water.
Some days we got lucky and spied a bikinied German girl
with a Speedoed German man,

getting naked together in a low spot

on the other side of the quarry,
sending us sand-gnat scurrying

        deep inside our caves

to catch our breath,
    crane our necks,
        and watch.

BASE EXCHANGE

My fashion maverick of a brother was
too damn secretive about
what he had in the bag, and he
hurried through the stairwell, tipping off
my nose-buried-in-the-newspaper father,
who smelled up-to-no-good blood
and sprang from the couch to expose
the operation.

And they fought a running battle
through the living room, down the hall,
past the bathroom, into a bedroom,
and things grew louder, heated, ugly,
until Chad opened the *"See, you asshole!"* bag
that contained a simple, black, sleeveless turtleneck
that zipped up the back.

And the Colonel was silent and stared
and moved his eyeballs back and forth over that shirt
at an unhealthy pace, like he might faint
or rupture a spleen, but he had made a
career of keeping it together, and
after confirming there were no secret codes
woven into the fabric
or cyanide capsules sewn into a seam,
he accused Chad of shoplifting.

EXPECTATIONS

My dad was changing clothes,
using the mirror
to button up a newly starched shirt,
standing at the end of the bed,
where he would lay out his uniform
each and every night,

> lining up his ribbons and awards
> in exact order with perfect spacing,
> centering his insignia and nametag
> according to published regulations,

when he told Chad and me that the purpose of his life
was to bring two people into the world
who were better than him.

And I had just
jerked off
and thought, oh well,
so much for that.

LOOK BEHIND YOU

This droopy-eyed, touch-of-home retarded kid
would pedal his legs something furious
and follow us around Rhein Main,
past the guardhouse and base theater,
up to the baseball field,
but never as far as the runways that

    landed

        troop

            transports and tankers and medevacs

        all   day.

And he would lick his lips
and laugh like a hyena,
telling us
Kathy gave him some delicious
drooly candy,
and he could eat a moon-sized
pizza,
and it was his birthday
every day,
all day.
And we had to wish him a happy birthday,
of course,
which made him cackle and ride around
fast in a tight circle.

But his all-time favorite
was to sneak up
when we weren't expecting—

        a droopy-eyed
        touch-of-home
        candy-drooling
        birthday-lying
        pizza-eating
        retarded kid—

to shout at the top of his lungs,

Look behind you!

Car coming!

LIBYA

White snowflake,
build-a-snowman snow days
somehow eluded us.
The snow sent us, long-faced, trudging
to the bus stop,
barely acknowledging each other,
emerging from the low stairwells,
and begging the gray clouds
for more.

But politics came through
on a no-buses-rolling,
> *school-is-canceled,*
> *go-back-to-bed,*
> *your-father-had-to-go-in-early,*
> *everything-is-fine*
> morning.

That day, Reagan served Gaddafi
an early-bird special
of high explosives, smothered in a
generous helping of "fuck you",
for the discotheque bombers who
murdered our GIs,
who were trying to kick it
on the dance floor.

BUSH

One endless summer-mischief day,
a rush of screeching security police
in freshly starched uniforms
converged at the back gate,

and we stopped skating
long enough to notice the wheeled marquee
next to the theater:

Greetings, Vice President Bush.

But the cops ignored us,
preoccupied with traffic and cigarette butts
and little American flags,

giving us time
and incentive
to rearrange the letters,
just as the first

        long, black, tinted limousine

rolled onto Rhein Main.

People exploded from the stairwells
into the street
        as if on cue,
all smiles,
        cheering,
with cookies,
like a herd of brainwashed Ivans,
except for the little American flags.

And we stood rag-tag sweaty,
covered in scabs,
wearing plaid shorts
and no shirts,
next to the sign that now read:

Vice President Gets Bush.

MOVIE NIGHT

Anticipating big action flown in from the States,
we smacked Jujubees and
gulped American soda pop
and looked around for people we knew
and people we were avoiding.

The projector guy fumbled and bumbled
with the big reels,
taking longer than usual,
making the full house of airmen and commanders,
spouses and children,
and a whole row of grocery baggers
restless and noisy, like there might be a riot.

But a scabby little skateboarder stood up

and walked to the front of the theater

and hopped onto the short wooden stage

and launched into

a series of poppin' and lockin'

with a backspin
and extra windmills.

(Grocery baggers love windmills.)

And by the time
the packed house
was roaring with applause,
the movie had started.

BACK GATE

It was just past midnight,
and we were late

    (barely)

after a night in Frankfurt.

And we were running up the hill
from the last German bus stop,
knowing the gate would be locked,
chained-up secure,
but we needed to see it like that
before starting the five-mile walk
to the front gate,
which stayed open all night.

And one of us yelled,
and one of us cursed,
and one of us kicked the fence,
and the gate …

Can you believe it?

… creaked slowly open.
And we jumped back
in total shock,
not believing it was

    unguarded, unlocked, unsecured.

And Muammar Gaddafi
could have led a camel train
through it, *nude*, no less,

carrying the entire
Red Army Faction
and ten thousand Soviet infantrymen,
and no one would have seen them
infiltrating
little America.
So we ran home,
barely making our curfew,
to tell our parents about our luck,
knowing
some security policeman's luck
had just run out.

School Days

ENGLISH TEACHER

During the usual laugh-slappy,
        grab-ass,
        between-class
        locker slamming,
I saw her—
hidden almost—
deep inside her classroom,
sitting in the dark,
looking older
        (and she was already old),
looking smaller
        (and she was already small),
just back from somewhere in the States
for a reason none of us knew.

And I tried to look away,
keep my head down,
fumble for a book I knew I didn't need.

But I couldn't get past her.
I never could.

So I crept in, nervous,
and said her name,
and she looked up, startled,
but welcomed me,
saying,

        It is like the Life Force
        is gone from your life,
        losing your father.

And we had never talked like that,
and I did not know what to say,
and she kept waiting for an answer.

But I had none and said I was sorry,
and she hugged me.

And because she lived alone
and was quick to anger
and dragged a leftover,
crooked hand
and a broken-up polio foot
back and forth to school
   as a child
      (and now, as an adult),

I left wondering
how many people had ever hugged her,
other than her father,
buried now, somewhere back in the States.

PEA HEAD

After the final bell,
this black guy with big front teeth
and a big mouth ...

Yo! My name is Pea Head! You will respect me, motherfucker!

... climbed onto the school bus and said,

What's up, Slick?

to the German driver,
who nodded,
even though his name was not *Slick*,
because everyone was *Slick*,
even the *motherfuckers* who didn't respect him.

And Pea Head stopped,
barely a step down the aisle,
and reached in his coat and pulled out
an X-ray he'd snuck from science class
of a chicken with a broken neck.

And people stopped talking
as he peered through it
and turned it slowly,
concentrating,
    turning
tongue-sticking-out concentrating,
                  turning
until finally the broken neck hung
perfectly at exactly the right angle,
and he thrust the X-ray high up

over his tiny round head
and shouted,

Yo!

I broke my dick!

GREASED BUNS

The Red Army Faction
got us again,
just down the street
from the barbed wire

        cordoning o
                  f
     t   f
     h
     e high school

blowing up the hot-dog stand,
sending wieners flying
and denying us
that touch of home
between third and fourth periods.

And even though we still had hamburgers,
that wasn't the point.

CREATIVE WRITING

A slitty-eyed, red-cheeked, hyena-laughing stoner
hung a full-sized poster of Bruce Dickinson,
sweating in spandex,
        grinding his junk on a mike stand,
between framed effigies of Chaucer and Shakespeare.

And we snickered because
old Mrs. Rotter,
        all of eighty-seven years,
didn't know any better.

And we kept her distracted
by knocking on our desks
to see how many times
she would answer the door.

Who's out there?

And we hurled fist-sized spitballs
soaked in cups of water,
that thunder-*slapped* against the blackboard
before dying a slow, droopy descent
        into the chalk tray.

What's so funny?

Until she agreed to take us to the park
        where the stoners bought hash
        in little black squares on shiny tin foil
        sold by Turks and slitty-eyed,
        red-cheeked, hyena-laughing Germans

to work on our writing,
and where on cue,
(Run!)
we ran away in different directions,
laughing and singing Iron Maiden songs,
while old Mrs. Rotter squinted
into the sun, waving her arm
like we were doing her a favor.

ANGELA

Despite bug eyes, buck teeth, and gangly legs,
she had tremendous self-confidence,
so I respected her.

And she was wearing her uniform,
JROTC combat boots and red ascot,
with her hair pulled back,
making her bug eyes
                buggier,
her buck teeth
                buckier,
when she volunteered
to take the stage.

And we were
hot-damn, *this-can't-be-happening*
electrified with a guffawing energy
as the music started, and Angela
launched into her first-ever African tribal dance,
with a thrashing and jerking
and a cartoon-leg kicking
that suddenly got the best of her.

And we gasped as she flailed her rubbery arms
and pounded her furious feet,
trying something—*anything*—to right the too-late dangerous tilt,
as she fell backwards into a stage light
that exploded in a bluish-white flash,
followed by a bolt-upright holy-hell thunderclap

    that triggered an auditorium-shaking shriek,
           as Angela

Combat boots
      Red ascot
            Buck teeth
                  Gangly legs
                        Bug eyes

tumbled off the stage
and into that place
where people go in high school
when they just want to die.

THE FRAU

She growled at us in her native tongue
and moved on large ankles,
frowning through the rows of desks,
making sure we paid attention:

    der, die, oder das.

But there were times she became
all-of-a-sudden
awkward
and stopped conjugating
and turned from the blackboard

    eins ... zwei ... drei ... gazoofa

before exploding into a finger-waving,
little Hitler,
hand-pounding tirade,
    damning Ivan
for what he'd done forty years ago
to her very own father,
a blitzkrieger, fighting honorably
vor den Vaterland
deep on the Eastern Front,
where he was captured
and marched to a prison camp
by barbarians
    who beat him
    and tortured him
    and starved him
    until he was all-the-way dead.

And when she was done, she would look away,
and no one would say anything
until after class,
once the bell rang,
and we were far enough down the hall.

And someone would look over
a shoulder before saying,

Hel-lo?

Can someone say Dachau?

AUTOBAHN

Her very American parents were uptight-nervous
about letting her take the family sedan
onto the autobahn,
but the three of us convinced them,
being National Honor Society members.

And as we waved a sugary good-bye
and rounded the corner through the back gate,

> I turned on the radio,
> *swished* the windshield wipers,
> cranked on the air conditioner,
> and activated the hazard lights,

distracting her by making her turn them all off
because I thought it was funny,
and she had just learned how to drive.

But we both got caught up in it,
and never noticed the cars had stopped
in the middle of the autobahn
until the person in the back seat
screamed bloody fucking murder,
and she stomped the brake,

        skid-d-d-ing
                and   squealing   and

(*somehow*)
                        barely stopping inches away
from being a news story.

And right then and there,
I inducted her into
the National Honor Society
for brand-new drivers who survive
stupid pranks played by asshole passengers.

Lonely

He was a crusty, old, bald-headed Texan,
teaching algebra,
and he had been there forever,
so they never messed with him
or asked him to take down the sign
above his classroom door:

Arbeit Macht Frei

And he lived by himself
somewhere in Frankfurt,
and he would sit at his desk after school
and talk about politics
or the stock market
or whatever.

   But he would ask me to sit on his lap,

      and he promised to knit me a sweater,

         and he held my hands for entirely too long.

But I liked him and talked to him,
never wanting to think it was weird,
only that he was lonely.

FRIEND

He was *All Europe* in three sports
and scored the hottest white girls
and sat with me on the bus after wrestling practice.

And I am sure we looked funny,
because he towered over me
and weighed twice what I did,
and people were heart-stoppingly terrified of him
because he would get drunk
and beat the hell out of Germans, Turks, and GIs,
sometimes all at the same time.

So after getting off the bus,

See you tomorrow.

the white kids would walk up behind me
and whisper,

What do you guys talk about?

I mean, really?

Cock Watcher

This crass girl, who was funny as hell
and smoked Marlboros,
goofed on us with this game
where she stuck her index finger
down by her crotch and called out,

Cock watcher!

whenever someone looked,
which made her laugh hysterically.

Until one day I waited for her
and snuck out my dong
while she lit a smoke
and puffed easily,
until she noticed,

Cock watcher!

which made her choke
and stumble angrily,

putting an immediate end
to our game.

SAY WHAT?

Lee the Brit came from England
but fancied himself American
after his mom married a GI.

But he still smoked fags
and loved a pint,
and the ladies loved him
because he talked sexy
and spiked his hair like Billy Idol.

And one afternoon,
riding home on the bus,
he got going
about riding some girl
back in England,
mesmerizing the rows
of wide-eyed Velcro-shoed boys
gripping their Trapper Keepers.

And from what I could gather,
this girl did not possess
his British sensibilities,

because without warning
or provocation

(to quote the proper Englishman,)

"She farted on me balls."

BAD KISSER

I hopped a train downtown
with a girl from Frankfurt, and we walked
through crowds of *damen und herren* to the opera
and ate ice cream with money I'd made
from sweeping out the stairwell.

And we ended up next to a fountain,

but before we kissed, she
took her hands from her pockets
and told me to quit looking at her mouth
        and into her eyes,
making me self-conscious and changing everything.

She kissed me with a smirk,
then never went downtown with me again.

SKEET

On Saturdays we woke early and carried shotguns
past the runways, which were busy ferrying men and materials
to the four corners of the earth.

And I was there the day my dad hit twenty-five in a row,
    when we filled his hat full of clay pigeons
        (to give it some weight),
    and folded over the bill
        (so the pigeons wouldn't fall out),
    and tossed it high into the air
        (so we wouldn't shoot each other),
    and then blasted the hell out of it
        (because that was what you did).

But after a while I started to feel pressure
to concentrate and focus and be more consistent,
so I quit and never went back,

deciding that, far more challenging
    and exhilarating

than shattering little orange disks with a shotgun,

        was a girl down the street named Jennifer.

DINNER

I worked up the nerve to ask Jennifer to dinner,
even though she barely knew my parents
and was just starting to laugh at my jokes.

But I thought my chances were good,
because my brother was off with a friend,
        so it wasn't like he could wreck it.

And when we all sat down,
I was ready with an ice-breaker,
        a NATO question I'd thought up
          to get the Colonel to talk,
to make the whole thing less awkward.

And he was pretty plugged in
and took the bait,
knowing he was taking it,
clearing his throat and swirling his Scotch,
before starting down the path I had planned …

        When in walked *Chad,*
        all sweaty from skateboarding,
        and I nearly choked
        and glared
        and tried to will him
            back outside,
                to his room,
                    to another planet,

just *go* somewhere else,
      and hurry up,

  but it was too late.

Chad listened for a minute
before rolling his eyes and cutting off the Colonel,

Come on—we never talk like this at dinner.

replacing the well-constructed analysis
with silverware scraping porcelain,
   ice cubes rattling in glass,
     and a roaring silence that Ivan could hear,
clear across the Iron Curtain.

COURTING

The first time I kissed Jennifer,
we stood outside her stairwell
in the concrete entryway,
next to the big brown fire door
        propped open by a wooden wedge.

And it was late,
and we were talking and laughing
until it grew quiet and still,
into that perfect
        no-going-back,
I-can't-believe-it's-actually-going-to-happen moment.

Except it was awkward
because we were such good friends,
and she made me feel so many things,
and I was desperate for it to work out.

I kissed her anyway,

and she made a not-ready effort
that sank me.

Then she turned too quickly
and collided with the door frame
before collecting herself
to go through it a second time,
without turning to acknowledge
both of her mistakes.

FINALLY

I never *really* gave up hope
because we lived on the same street,
inside the same barbed-wire fence,

        rode the same bus,
        took the same classes,
        ran with the same crowd.

And it's nothing you can force,
no matter how much you want
it to happen.

And it's almost like you decide
it's not going to happen,
and you quit trying
        to walk to the bus at the same time
        or leave an open seat next to you in class.

Then that magical, someone-pinch-me day
finally arrives,
        where she does want to kiss you.

And things explode into
a full-fledged courtship,
where you discover
an entire world exists
outside the barbed-wire fence
of castles and cathedrals
and tucked-away cafés,

where it's just you and her,
and time stands still,

and the world aches
with incredible possibility.

L.O.S.T.

L.O.S.T.

About that time I joined a scream-your-head-off punk band
with American guys from high school;
we wanted to make a statement
against all the *-isms* plaguing society,
so we called ourselves

      Lots of Social Tolerance

which made the coolest acronym
and gave us hope for the future.
And there was talk of changing the world—
      serious we-can-do-it talk—
until one day Eric the Bassist and Joe the Drummer
started making fun of Turks
and plunged the band into an identity crisis.

And because good old-fashioned
punk acronyms don't grow on trees,
      (and poseurs really, really suck),
we knew what was best,
and right then and there, between songs,
we became

      Lack of Social Tolerance

          One ... Two ... Three ... Four ...

and rejoined the revolution.

JOE D'LONRA

The drummer von L.O.S.T. wore
tight jeans and smoked smokes
and grew his hair long
and had a wicked fastball,
and got kicked out of another band
before founding L.O.S.T.
and telling his dad
he didn't want to play baseball.

He told me in his stairwell,
after we watched porn with Eric the Bassist.

> All of us sitting patiently,
> with pillows covering our junk,
> waiting until we could stand up again.

But there was no hiding anything
when Joe started spelling his last name backwards,
after he came home early
and caught his old man in the kitchen,

> *Dude, you are not going to believe this …*

bent over some random chick from the bowling team.

> *Wow.*

> *Yeah.*

> *Isn't Mrs. Arnold on that team, too?*

Eric the Bassist

He kicked ass at trombone before picking up a bass,
and he called himself
Dave Slider von L.O.S.T.
and spent summers weed-whacking the tarmac
to keep the flight line unencumbered,

>as scores of aircraft
>touched down,
>>unloaded,
>
>reloaded,
>and lifted off,
>>never staying long
>>to keep Ivan guessing.

And he would come home with grass in his hair, ears, teeth …
a good soldier waging war
>for God and country.

And we would sit together
behind his stairwell,
just inside the barbed wire,
where he would light a smoke
and talk about going double-platinum,
knowing we never would.

But he was an American, dammit,
fighting a war he could not win,
and he needed something—*anything*—
to walk the tarmac another day.

PICKLES

Bill the guitarist could kick anybody's ass
down in Sachsenhausen,
where people threw sucker-punches
and fought anyone and everyone.

And the day Metallica came to town,
he skipped school and
sucked down too many beers.
He chased them with
McDonald's cheeseburgers
that he hardly chewed,
stuffing them easily into his mouth.

And when the lights went down
and the crowd erupted,
Bill began puking whole pickles,
      little green land mines
that swept the legs out from under
a gaggle of leather-clad metal-heads,

letting the air out of their
otherwise perfectly synchronized

        head-banging,
           hair-slinging,
              air-guitar,
                  I-wanna-rock!

routine.

TOENAIL

On a ski hill near Munchen, I wore ski boots
        one size too big
and launched myself off
        one jump after another,
slamming my toes hard
        with each wobbly landing,
but impressing the girls …
        I think.

It cost me a toenail
that worked its way off
with help from a pair of pliers.

And after swishing it
with clear nail polish that I got from my mom,
I showed it to Dave Slider von L.O.S.T.,
and because we were dangerous
and totally punk rock,
        (totally!)
he used it to play his bass.

HARDCORE

As far as we could tell, Dave Slider and I
were the only Americans in the entire crowd
of mohawks and black lipstick,
which made us all the more cool
and gave us bragging rights
and finally the courage to lock elbows
and push into the mosh pit,
as Alien Sex Fiend turned the place
into a sea of churning bodies.

And as we moved deeper into the fray
of Frankfurt's writhing underground,
a leather elbow smashed Slider
        square in the nose,
squirting blood everywhere,
forcing us to fight our way
to the shit-stained bathroom,
where he washed his face
and crammed toiled paper into his nostrils.

And not two songs into the show,
we agreed that we were not that hardcore
and left to get ice cream.

New Line-Up

We didn't talk about it for days
when Dave Slider got shipped
back to the States, because
it reminded us of what we were
always trying to forget ...

>that we weren't from anywhere, *really*,
>and didn't have hometowns
>or know our extended families ...

and guys like Dave Slider were our extended family,
which is why it hurt like hell to see him go.

So we felt sorry for ourselves
and pecked around in the dirt,
until Guido and Buddha arrived,
making three suddenly five.

And we skipped school one day
and drove east through the snow to a tiny studio
a hand-grenade's throw from the Iron Curtain,
where we recorded new songs
that we mailed to New Jersey,
where Dave Slider sat in a bedroom
in a house with a white picket fence
in the middle of suburbia
and followed along on his bass,
reconnecting with the punk-ass derelicts who
lived in stairwells with big brown fire doors
propped open with wooden wedges,

in the middle of a barbed-wire fence
that had felt so much like family—and home.

PROM NIGHT

We partied all over Frankfurt
and it was my first night without a curfew,
and we ended up in a bad part of town,
where a homeless guy came at us
shouting with a diseased mouth.

And when he stumbled too close,
Bill said to D'lonra,

> *I go low; you go high.*

And he hit the concrete
and did not move.

And I looked once
to see if he was dead
but then kept going,
because it was prom night,

> and we were
>> *buying ...*
>>> *a stairway ...*
>>>> *to heaven ...*

HITTING THE ROAD

Goggles

I was sitting on the dock next to my brother
as the sun eased behind the Alps,
and the wind picked up, making us shudder.
We reached for our towels, but my brother
hooked his necklace on the dock
and tore away the Greek coin
my father had brought back from Athens.

And as it
    S
     A
      N
       K
    I
     N
    T
     O
            the lake,

we scurried from side to side
on the old wooden slats,
screaming and pointing.

He's gonna be pissed.

    I think I see it!

But the water under the dock was deep and muddy and full of reeds,
which became impossible to see in without sunlight, so we said

to hell with our goggles, and Chad hung his head
and then marched bravely around the lake to take his lumps.

    (He was always braver than me.)

But later that night, we were glad to have goggles
in the hotel pool, where a German frolicked
in the deep end with two women, groping and rubbing
and turning the three of them into a mass of
    writhing,
        kissing,
            laughing,
fogging-up-my-goggles good time.

HAIRCUT

Before a family trip to Paris,
the Colonel ordered us
to stop screwing with our hair
because we looked like hooligans.

But Chad never listened
or took the guy seriously,
which was why I was surprised to find him
outside our stairwell,
crying,
        (sobbing, really)
each back-shaking wail
echoing through the building.

And he was wearing a hooded sweatshirt,
and he said he was only messing around,
which was odd because he was

bald

except for perfectly normal bangs,
and we were supposed to leave for Paris
in the morning.

    Holy shit.

The Colonel was going to be pissed.

Mom looked nervously
at the clock and wrung her hands,
calculating his arrival,
not knowing what to say or do.

But I did.
I laughed
        and laughed and laughed and laughed,
until we were all crying.

MEET AND GREET

On a whirlwind *See Italy in Three Days* tour,
we rode a bus to Herculaneum
with this little Hispanic kid
who toted a brown Cabbage Patch doll
named Bob.

Why not "Roberto"?

And halfway to the ruins
I decided to make Bob's acquaintance
and turned in my seat.

But before I could say hello,
the little Hispanic bastard smashed me
a neck-snapping good one
square on the nose
with Bob's hard plastic head,
forcing me to whirl back around
and wipe away tears,
as Chad cracked up
and I saw Pompeian red.

Digging

After mimicking the final contortions
of the bodies entombed in ash,
I thought about a time in the States
when I'd thrown a pencil three rows up.
It had landed softly and perfectly
between the fleshy ass cheeks
of a heavy kid with thick glasses,
who always had plumber's butt
and never did his Latin homework.

And after the pencil found its mark,
he reached deep between his puffies,

    way

        way

            down,

and rummaged around in the back of his pants,
before finally grabbing it and bringing it
slowly to the surface—
like it was a newly recovered artifact
from a lost civilization.

All while the teacher

    amo'd

        amas'd

            amot'd

and remained oblivious to the archeology
taking place in the sweaty ass crack
of one of her lesser gladiators.

Butt Lint

Chad did the unthinkable
and flew to the USSR
and saw Ivan up close
with a group of American kids
and a weary chaperone.

And they drank their asses off
aboard Aeroflot's creaky jets.

And Chad must have stayed drunk,
because he came back
claiming that Ivan wasn't a
      two-headed,
           fire-breathing
                Commie

   (with nukes).

But I didn't believe him
and was sure they had gotten to him.

   The power of propaganda!

And to honor his return,
I used the inlaid jar
he'd bought me in Tashkent
for something special,

filling it each night
with whatever had accumulated
between my American ass cheeks
before going to bed.

ANDORRA

We rode through the Pyrenees
with this Puerto Rican guy,
who worked with the Colonel
and steered with his knee,
    strumming an air guitar
      to "Black Magic Woman."

And he was telling us about
getting shot down
    in Vietnam,

    and his son listened quietly
    and looked out the window,
      then cocked his head
        in the direction of Andorra
    and couldn't look away,
      like he and Santana
      were hearing it all
      for the first time.

And we saw the thick purple scar
where a bullet had gone through him
after tearing up his helicopter as it
hovered over a hot LZ,

    half a world away,
    a generation ago,
    before he had a son,

which fired me up way more than some
crappy little tax haven
nestled between Spain and France.

UGLY AMERICAN

We boarded buses and rolled
through the barbed wire,
and woke up in Prague,
where we met some Czechs
with big hair and funny accents,
who whispered about Moscow
        because they hated Ivan
           more than we did.
They looked over their shoulders
before shouting,

    But we love America!

And they wanted to know:

    How is Michael Jackson? We love Michael Jackson!
    How much is a pair of Levis? We love blue jeans!
    What is cool? We love cool!

And I almost said,

    "Cool" is not your imitation Bobo tennis shoes,

but I bit my tongue and remembered my manners
and looked over my shoulder before saying,

    Michael is fine, and you sure do have a nice city.

Dutch Ducks

We rode wooden skiffs through the foggy sunrise
to square boxes of shrubbery
that grew in shallow water,
where the fleshy-faced guides spoke
pidgin English and worked the hell
out of the duck call.

But my father had grown up
killing ducks in North Dakota,
and he stood up first inside the shrubs,
turning two ducks limp
with as many shots,
making the pidgin guides smile broadly
and shake their heads
and slap my father on the back,
leaving nothing lost in translation.

HOMESICK

After trimming the tree in my senior year,
we all started crying
except for the Colonel,
who lit a cigarette,
while my mom wiped her eyes
and told me how much
they loved me,
and I could always come home,
whenever I wanted …

which was about the weirdest thing
I had ever heard, because
where the hell else would I go?

Auf Wiedersehen

After graduating from Frankfurt American High School in May 1988, I waved good-bye to the Colonel as he boarded an aircraft bound for the States. The needs of the military required him to ship out ahead of us. Until we boarded our own plane, my mother, Chad, and I lived out of suitcases in the same base hotel that we had evacuated three years earlier. This time we did not suffer any bomb threats, and for the last few days in country, I spent every waking hour with Jennifer.

But a funny thing happened on the way to the Flughafen. Before climbing into the taxi, before saying a final *auf wiedersehen*, I felt transformed by the barbed-wire bubble known as Rhein Main, where machine guns and military aircraft reminded me every day that "out there," the world seethed with adult anger. And even though I preferred making love to war, now that I was finally shipping back to the States, I suddenly realized I was a soldier myself. However, my cold war had been a three-year war for normalcy.

So as the taxi pulled away, I waved good-bye to Jennifer and then wiped away my tears, realizing I had done it. I had survived. I also realized I couldn't have done it on my own, and as the taxi drove through Rhein Main's front gate and onto the autobahn, I thought about everyone with whom I had shared the hottest of times during the coldest of wars.

978-0-595-44233-1
0-595-44233-1

Printed in the United States
91974LV00005B/298/A